TESTIMONIALS

Why listen to me? Listen to what my clients say about me. Then follow the tips and tactics in this book and start collecting testimonials like these!

Adrian R'Mante

CEO, Actor, Director, Producer - www.CGTV.LA

"My name is Adrian R'Mante and I am the owner of CGTV in Hollywood, CA. You may remember me as "Esteban" for over 7 years on Disney's "The Suite Life of Zack and Cody". I engaged Gia Heller and The Social Media Masters in October of 2015. People talk a big talk in the marketing game I have come to realize, so when Gia came in, I did not give her a ton of credit, in fact it was my brother that told me she was a superstar and that we needed her. Hiring Gia was one of the best decisions I have made yet for my business. Yes, Gia has all of the skills necessary to be a good marketer. Writing and branding skills, knowing the Facebook algorithms and how to find and attract your target. But she has more than that. She has a passion for my business, which is very rare to find. She acts as if she is your business partner, not just your Marketing Director.

Gia successfully markets us in Malaysia, Singapore, Guadalajara, London, California, Texas, Phoenix and anywhere else we decide to host our events/ auditions. We have always spent significant ad money on Facebook, but since Gia, the results have more than doubled without doubling what we are spending. She knows exactly how the internet works and she masters it. And she is my right hand man. If I text her at night from Singapore or in the morning from Hollywood, she is always there for me. She knows her worth and she still doesn't gouge her clients for money. She is the fairest pricing my firm has come across with the wildest results, ever.

Gia has also helped us with understanding how our website and blog need to interact as many times as possible with the search engines to come up for keywords that you want to be found for. In fact, we had parents that had never purchased our program leaving negative reports about us at Rip Off Report. Gia has and continues to create over 20 amazing success story blogs per month on our testimonials of stars that have made it on major television shows and movies because of us. Which gives us the opportunity to prove our successes to parents doing their due diligence.

Let me be clear, I am not easy to please and I am very hard to win over, but after working with her for 8+ months I know that Gia is reliable, dependable, passionate about my business and highly skilled and we are grateful to have her as such an integral part of CGTV. We see Gia as a legacy player. If you are even questioning hiring her, you just aren't listening."

*   *   *

John Scherer

Founder of The Video Professor & CEO of www.CanlessAir.com

"With nearly 1B in products sold, I know a little something about marketing. And in my years of experience, I have met very few professionals that I can say the same about. Gia is one of them. She is an excellent brainstormer, creative thinker and knows how to market and sell a product and/or service using her common sense and digital acumen. I strongly suggest Gia and The Social Media Masters. My latest endeavor, Canless Air has her creative talents at the helm of our Facebook page www.Facebook.com/CanlessAirSystem."

*   *   *

Cory Michael Sanchez
Mojo Global Marketing (CEO, Co-Founder)

"I love the Social Media Masters and Gia Heller. She's an amazing person and fiercely passionate about the results her clients get. She is always on the front line of what is going on in social media and breaks news on new developments. If you're tired of wasting your money and time with social media or not getting the results you are looking for then do yourself a favor and get into her program because they will give you the engagement and exposure you're looking for. I have known Gia for 7 years and she is always the person I call for all things Facebook."

*   *   *

Hessam Rahimian
Car Dealership Owner

"I have owned a car dealership for over 25 years. Before that, I ran the marketing for the largest Chevrolet retailer in the world. It was after my one-hour consult with Gia Heller that I came to realize that I know very little when it comes to marketing. Gia is the queen and Goddess of not only Facebook, but marketing in general! Thank you Gia!"

*   *   *

Randy Keith
CEO, Musician at www.PremierePianoShows.com

"From content creation and branding to the most efficient methods of taking posts viral, Gia Heller and the Social Media Masters truly are the epitome in the industry. The network of timely resources they provide is an invaluable resource for the small business owner not just keeping up with, but outpacing, the big guns."

*   *   *

Robert Martinez

CEO at www.Facebook.com/CoachesCoach

"The numbers don't lie... Before working with Gia and The Social Media Masters, registrations from Facebook for my webinars were at 23%, after 6 months of working with Gia, registrations from Facebook have doubled, now at 46%... If you want to reach more people on Facebook, you need to work with Gia!!"

*   *   *

Read more at www.Facebook.com/TheSocialMediaMasters/reviews

THE STARTUP ENTREPRENEUR

100 Tips and Tactics to implement NOW for Serious income!

GIA HELLER

JONES MEDIA PUBLISHING

The Startup Entrepreneur: 100 Tips and Tactics to implement NOW for Serious income! Copyright © 2016 by Gia Heller.

Jones Media Publishing
10645 N. Tatum Blvd. Ste. 200-166
Phoenix, AZ 85028
www.JonesMediaPublishing.com

Disclaimer:
The author strives to be as accurate and complete as possible in the creation of this guide, notwithstanding the fact that she does not warrant or represent at any time that the contents within are accurate due to the rapidly changing nature of the Internet.

While all attempts have been made to verify information provided in this publication, the Publisher assumes no responsibility for errors, omissions, or contrary interpretation of the subject matter herein. Any perceived slights of specific persons, peoples, or organizations are unintentional.

In practical advice books, like anything else in life, there are no guarantees of income made. Readers are cautioned to rely on their own judgment about their individual circumstances to act accordingly. This book is not intended for use as a source of legal, business, accounting or financial advice. All readers are advised to seek services of competent professionals in legal, business, accounting, and finance field.

Edited by: Meria Heller & Vicki Bezio
ISBN: 978-0-9973408-6-0 paperback

This book is dedicated to __all__ the people that have helped me physically, emotionally, mentally, financially and spiritually on my journey.

TO MY GRANDMOTHER, **Leah**, for producing five amazing women that raised me with unconditional love. Thank you to my mother and aunts for instilling the entrepreneurial spirit in me from a very early age.

To my good friends and chosen family, **Peter and Kim Denton**, for opening their hearts and home to my family after the real estate crash keeping us from being homeless and giving us a safe and loving home. It was in this home that I was able to build my businesses from the ground up. Without them I would have been forced to take a job to feed my family. I am eternally grateful. I love you both.

To my daughters, **Jenna and Jessk**a, who never complained when we lost it all. Thanks for believing in me even when I didn't believe in myself. Thanks for never asking me "Why don't you just get a job mom?" If you had I might never have built any of this.

To my Millennial husband, **Michael Howard**, who has taught me more patience in 4 years than I have learned in a lifetime.

To my mother, **Meria**, a published author, super busy news reporter and perfectionist for providing me support editing while I was in Italy even though it would have been so much easier to say "I wish I could but I just don't have the time." Thank you for making the time for what is important to you. Me. And to **Vicki Bezio, Jenna McKenna & Michael Howard** for reading & helping me with the final edits!

To **Sissy** who gave me expensive spa pedicures and manicures, gas money, and even made sure I ate during the roughest times while I built my empire. Not to mention the emergency loans! Thank you for your unconditional love and support through the Kool Aid days.

To **Top Hat Terry**, my right hand man and teacher at The Social Media Masters, for bringing amazing content to our students and always having my back in both physical and virtual realms.

To **Bill Walsh**, my Rock star mentor, who cared more about how much money I was charging my clients than I did. You taught me how to value myself while continuing to provide my clients with more than they paid for.

* * *

CONTENTS

PREFACE

I WAS QUOTED IN the book *Think and Grow Rich for Women* by Sharon Lechter with the *Napoleon Hill Foundation* as saying "It's difficult to be an 'expert' at anything if you do 'everything'". I firmly believe that specializing in your natural born talent brings not only riches but immense pleasure as well.

I have been doing social media since its inception in 1995, from the moment I saw it I was hooked. Like a fresh love affair, I could not get enough. I worked faster than most employees thus I could get most of my work done in half a business day and still have hours to spend on social media. In fact, I would say that I was addicted to social media!

From the moment my babies went to sleep I would sit for hours in front of my computer fascinated with all the strangers in front of me that I would have never met before. In fact, I met my youngest daughter's father in a Phoenix Chatroom and my now 19-year-old daughter is probably one of the first internet babies born in 1997.

My areas of expertise are in marketing, sales and efficiency systems. Whatever you are doing in your business I can make you harder, faster and stronger by using technology. Ever since I was a teen, I have always earned a decent living because I provided system and solutions to bosses that made them a lot of money. I even convinced myself that my bosses' passions were my own until 2003 when I left corporate America to become an Entrepreneur. I was quite successful internationally. I used social media (Myspace specifically) to build relationships and earn the trust of my international real estate clients to whom I sold millions of dollars in properties to. But I never loved real estate the way I did social media.

After losing it all I did what most people do, I went back to what I knew — real estate. I joined James Robinson at Phoenix Realty Advisors in Phoenix, Arizona where I painfully learned the in's and outs of commercial office leasing. I was mathematically challenged and poor James had to train me ten times longer than anyone else on the spreadsheets. But, that wasn't the worst part of the job. The worst part of the job was cold calling in three piece suits in 117-degree Phoenix summers. Returning to my car that was hot enough to bake cookies in after being rejected time and time again got very old very fast. When I told James that there HAD to be a better way to market a business he suggested that I start a referral/networking group. I rolled my eyes while pretending to shove a finger down my throat. Another "networking" group? Kill me, now.

I told James that networking groups were places that old, fat, balding, lonely men went to torture vivacious, energetic girls that like to hustle. He told me to create my own then and to grow it one person at a time, one from each industry. I took his advice. I created a group called Arizona Women Networking. At first, it was just me, my mother and Chiropractor Dr. Karen Jacobson. From there I brought in a commercial real estate attorney and kept growing. I just want to be clear that I did not start a woman's group because I am a feminist. I figured if I was going to start a networking group it was going to be effective and productive.

While I was researching networking groups one thing that really stood out to me was that women do 80% of all networking. At first, I thought that number was absurd. But, then I thought about it. If I tell a man "Wow,

I love your new haircut" a typical response would be "thanks" from said male. However, when I say the same sentence to a female I have a much higher chance of her going on a tangent about her hairdresser, how much she pays, how long she has been going and how much she loves him. You see, she is a walking, talking, living, breathing referral for her stylist, dentist, gynecologist and you name it! Women love to nurture and part of nurturing is connecting people to what they need. The group turned out to be a huge success. We were featured in the *Arizona Republic* business section on the front page as well as a 9pm news segment with Beverly Kidd from *AZ Family* broadcast to the greater Phoenix area. We went from 3 women around a table to over 180 members in the first 18 months.

Why so popular with over 800 networking groups in the valley at the time? We were the only group teaching and promoting social media. It was not an accepted mainstream marketing tool and most business owners declined getting involved. In fact, many better known marketers in town said I was a joke promoting Facebook as a professional way to market a business. My engaged clients and members are beating their top local and Fortune 500 competitors in engagement on Facebook. Now, I work from home and have a smile on my face all of the day. I take annual trips and months of vacation to balance the mad hours I work as an entrepreneur and life is beautiful. Yours can be too.

This book is a collection of tips I wish I knew when I started this journey, I hope they help you find the strength to follow your passion.

* * *

ARE YOU THINKING about, or currently in the early stages of starting a business? Perhaps you are a few years deep into it but not yet getting the results you expected? If you are unable to figure out why nothing is working this book is for you!

This book will give you tips and tactics to not only help you succeed in business but in life as well. You see, either all of your life works or none of it works. I can assure you I have lived it, and it is the truth. In fact, if you implement only some of the ideas in this book there is nowhere for you or your business to go but up. People have repeatedly asked me how I got to where I am today from losing it all and living on food stamps. These are the practical steps I took to change my life and realize this success.

* * *

CHAPTER 1

Why Own a Small Business & How Do I Start?

IT'S PATRIOTIC TO OWN A SMALL BUSINESS

AMERICA IS STRONGEST when Americans own small businesses. If you really want to help your country, you are going to have to help yourself first. There has never been a wider array of small businesses to choose from. From Uber to coffee shops, America needs you. In fact, those of us that can successfully start and maintain our own businesses can help others do the same. This also provides strength and stability to our communities. If you were born with capabilities, you have a responsibility to show up strong, succeed and lead the path for others.

DO WHAT YOU LOVE & LOVE WHAT YOU DO

YOU CAN MAKE money many different ways. Why not do what you LOVE and fill your life with joy? Getting paid for something you would do for free is one of the most fulfilling experiences in the world. For example, I was the top realtor broker with CBRE. Even while making plenty of money, I didn't LOVE real estate. Social media started off as my hobby which went on for ten years, and now I do social media for a living. Find your passion and know it can be monetized somehow.

NICHE IT UP

LIKE MY QUOTE in Think and Grow Rich says, pick ONE thing and do it exceptionally well! In business, being specific is where all the money is at. For example, I own a full service digital marketing company. We provide many services to our clients. However, I only provide the copywriting and Facebook personally. All of the rest is outsourced to other experts working on my team. Do what you do best and outsource the rest.

STOP GIVING ADVICE – START CONSULTING

THIS WAY WHEN they don't listen you have something in exchange for your time. No matter the subject, if you are constantly giving out advice to others and getting nothing in return, stop! Unfortunately, advice often falls upon deaf ears. As a consultant, I will tell you that even PAID FOR advice sometimes falls onto deaf ears. Stop giving advice for free and start advising for profit. If they truly respect and value your opinion they will hire you.

BE A UNICORN

AFTER ALL, YOU ARE a Unicorn. There is no one like you on the planet. You have ZERO competition. So start acting like it. Figure out what you do better than anyone else. Create a solution to a problem that affects many. Mark Zuckerberg created the largest and most versatile platform in the world connecting people, ideas and places. What is YOUR big idea or what is your simple solution to a widespread problem? Either can make you a star.

HAVE A BUSINESS PLAN

BUT, DON'T BE so in love with it that you can't evolve if and when you need to. If you would rather DIE than plan, hire or barter with someone that can help. There are many free online tools that can help. You can even find books like Business Plans for Dummies that can guide you through the steps of creating and following a business plan. Sometimes entrepreneurs are so enamored with their own idea that they can lose objectivity. Having a business plan will minimize unfocused and untargeted activities and keep you moving forward.

HAVE A PLANNING PROCESS

HAVING A BUSINESS plan is just the first step. Now, you must set goals, priorities, deadlines, and routinely measure your progress. Think of your plan as a living breathing organism and not concrete. Every day or every week this plan could change and will change as you come into challenges and triumphs that are unexpected. If you do not like the progress you are seeing set a course of correction. And, always remember to prioritize your list. If 30 items are a "priority," that means there really is no priority.

THESE BOOTS WERE MADE FOR FINANCING

BOOTSTRAPPING (SELF-FINANCING) IS popular among startups because most people do not have the savings or business credit necessary for the basic costs of starting and operating a business. Even if you seek outside cash from banks, the first thing they want to know is how much of your own cash you are risking. If you don't have enough faith to put your money where your mouth is why should they? Some people dip into savings, retirement, real estate equity, or extra vehicles. You can always trade services through a reputable barter company. No matter what the scenario, where there is a will, a way.

CHAPTER 2

Invest Time in Education & Knowledge

BE CLAIRVOYANT

I DON'T MEAN BEING a palm reader. Stay 5-10 years forward when researching and learning about new technologies in the marketplace. Be an early adapter. I was called "crazy" because I saw Facebook marketing as an effective tool 5-10 years before Fortune 500 companies utilized it. This time allowed me to build a presence and a reputation as a leader in the industry. Be at the forefront of your industry's evolution.

TAKE TYPING LESSONS

I HAVE WORKED WITH over 3,000 business owners and entrepreneurs and one thing evident in many is the snail's pace at which they type and navigate on their computer. Taking online typing lessons can help reduce your production time by 1-2 hours or more daily. When I was in corporate America my bosses paid me double the salary because I did twice the work my colleagues did in half the time.

LEARN HOW TO NAVIGATE YOUR COMPUTER

MANY ENTREPRENEURS LACK basic computer skills. It is hard to teach someone INTERNET marketing when they barely know how to use the keyboard and mouse pad. What takes the average skilled computer user 10 minutes takes them one hour. Everything is hard. You are frustrated so you quit right before the payday. If you plan on being a small business owner grow your technological skills or have very deep pockets to hire staff that can make up for it.

BUSINESS IS A MARATHON, NOT A SPRINT

WITH THE RIGHT training you can sprint marathons. The amount of time you spend learning and implementing is typically tied to what you are earning. Make sure your trainers have a proven track record prior to cutting that check for best results.

CHAPTER 3

Habits, Lifestyle & Mindset

DITCH YOUR ADDICTIONS

TIME IS MONEY so be very cautious where you spend it. Ten hours a week spent on Fantasy Football plus 10 hours a week watching games creates a 20-hour deficit from your work week. If something other than your business is taking up the bulk of your free time you picked the wrong passion. Go back to the drawing board and figure out how to monetize something you love as much as your addictions. Or, how you can incorporate something you love into your current business.

Gia Heller

CANCEL CABLE

GET HULU, NETFLIX, Amazon Prime and/or Apple TV. You will watch less, spend less, and only watch the shows you love. Consider turning off the news. The stories are dark and fear based and will not enhance your life. Focus your time and energy on personal and professional advancement instead.

DUMP ALCOHOL & PRICEY COFFEE SHOPS

SMALL BUSINESS OWNERS who complain about a lack of funds to market their business should do an honest self-assessment of their expenditures. If you don't have the money for marketing, but you have the money for bar tabs, pricey coffees and cigarettes, you have a problem. Invest in your marketing, not another habit.

GET YOUR ZZZS

L IKE ELECTRONICS, WE function our best when fully charged. Getting by on four hours of sleep isn't a testament to your physical strength or endurance. It is only a testament to your will. Lack of sleep takes away from your overall well-being. Insufficient sleep can lead to obesity, increased risk of heart disease, and even early death. Get your sleep and you'll work more productively. Put down all electronics about 2-4 hours prior to bed time. If possible sleep with your cell phone in another room.

BE JOYFUL

Y OU'RE GOING TO be very busy for the next five years growing your business. However, you should still take the time to smell the roses. Check out a museum, see a play, listen to some music, rent a bike, read a book in a park, and make new friends. No matter what you decide, do something. "I wish I had a few more hours to work" said no one, ever, on their deathbed.

MEDITATION

MEDITATE DAILY, EVEN if you're not into yoga and like the taste of champagne. It increases grey matter in areas of your brain related to memory and thought. Meditation also increases brain volume specifically in the areas of emotion regulation, positive emotions and self-control. As a Type A personality and lifetime insomniac, it was guided meditation and hypnosis that kept me from being hospitalized for lack of sleep. I find that using guided meditations by Michael Sealey works great and can be found on YouTube for free.

TAKE BREAKS

I GET IT YOU'RE on a roll and you want to power through. You want that kind of momentum however; you can still take a 1-minute break. We need to step away from the computer sometimes. Stand up, roll your neck, shoulders and wrists. Bend over and back up again. Drink water. Just this simple quick break will improve your blood flow and give you more energy to continue.

SCHEDULE YOUR NEXT VACATION

THE MINUTE YOU get home from your vacation, schedule the next. A very wealthy boss once taught me this. He said that as humans we need something to look forward to and work towards. Having a vacation in sight can help you focus on the task in front of you right now instead of dreaming about the "what ifs." If you are building your business this is a time for frugal vacations which can be adventurous and rewarding.

EXERCISE IN NATURE

THE GYM HAS benefits but the outdoors has more. Studies report people are happier when surrounded by nature on a regular basis. For example, there is a difference in the activity of bikers when they are on a stationary bike in a gym versus riding outside. A recent biking study proved that people who bike outside go harder and have a higher chance of repeating the activity for years to come. Many people that are not picture perfect avoid the gym due to self-confidence issues. Wall-to-wall mirrors and gym patrons can actually be de-motivators in exercising. Nature never judges.

CALM, COOL & COLLECTED

PEOPLE DO BUSINESS with people they like and trust. If you're having a hard time with remaining calm during difficult situations at work with clients or vendors, it is time to consider ways to reduce your stress and change your mindset so that you can embody leadership during tough times. It is easy to stay calm when things are going your way but your ability to maintain your composure during chaos proves what you are really made of and will ultimately decide how long the chaos prevails.

EXUDE ENTHUSIASM

MOODS ARE CONTAGIOUS so why not choose one that inspires others around you. What does Tony Robbins have that you don't? Enthusiasm, in spades. In fact, he is so enthusiastic that I believe that alone creates a ripe environment for his followers to blossom in. When I look at the TOP paying careers from commercial real estate to yacht sales, these guys and gals all have several things in common. They are charming, gregarious, outgoing and enthusiastic. Most top earners are. So stop whining & start shining.

BE CRAZY

DRAW OUTSIDE THE lines, do something no one has ever thought to do before. When I started talking about Facebook as a marketing tool, people said I was "crazy" because no one else was doing it. Now, thousands of people are creating careers that revolve around Facebook Marketing. This is one of my favorite quotes on the subject by one of my favorite entrepreneurs.

"Here's to the crazy ones. The misfits. The rebels. The troublemakers. The round pegs in the square holes. The ones who see things differently. They're not fond of rules. And they have no respect for the status quo. You can quote them, disagree with them, glorify or vilify them. About the only thing you can't do is ignore them. Because they change things. They push the human race forward. While some may see them as the crazy ones, we see genius. Because the people who are crazy enough to think they can change the world, are the ones who do."

~ STEVE JOBS

CELEBRATE THE WINS

NOT JUST THE big ones, but the little ones as well. After all it is the accumulation of little wins that make up the larger goal. As we celebrate each success our body wants to come up with more solutions to more challenges to receive more rewards. In short, don't wait to reach your goal to be proud of yourself. Be proud of yourself with each step you take on the road to success. Treat yourself.

Gia Heller

GROW THICKER SKIN

IN BUSINESS WE have to do what is necessary. Unfortunately, necessary doesn't always feel good. For example; you catch your niece stealing from the company. It is certainly not a nice feeling to fire her but a necessary action. Unfortunately, growth always involves pain. It also means giving something up. We have to give something up to get something new. Often, what we have to give up is an addiction to making comfortable decisions instead of the needed decision.

BE A GREAT COACH

AS A COACH I can tell you that only 10-20% of those you serve will take your advice and follow through on their commitments. I have also learned that the ones you think will work hard, won't. The ones you feared would fail could be your brightest and best. In short, coach, train, advise and serve as if they are ALL listening. When you do, more of them will.

WORKING LONGER ISN'T THE ANSWER

STANFORD PROFESSOR JOHN Pencavel proved something that I have always thought to be true - being a martyr working insane hours on your business doesn't mean you are as productive as you think you are. In fact, Professor Pencavel performed a study in 2014 with data collected from laborers during World War I. His findings were that those who put in 70 hours per week were no more productive than their co-workers working 56 hours per week. In short, spend time creating systems and you can work less and produce more.

FORGET ABOUT THE COMPETITION

PEOPLE SEEM MORE concerned about losing business to competitors than anything else. They never even ask themselves if the opposition is doing better work than they are. Worry less about competitors stealing business from you and worry more about competitors being better than you. The scarcity mindset is illogical. The planet is overpopulated so there is plenty of business for everyone. I don't worry about competitors. In fact, I train people in my own industry.

BE AN OPTIMIST

9 9% OF SUCCESS is believing it IS possible. Here are a few reasons to be an optimist. Not only does optimism make you feel better it can actually make you healthier. You have heard of "Don't sweat the small stuff" but did you know that negative thinking produces more of the stress hormone, cortisol, which side effects range from heart attacks to depression. Not naturally cheery and optimistic? Don't worry like anything else optimism is a skill that can be practiced and honed. You can even fake it until you make it!

BE TOLERANT

NO MATTER WHAT your religious beliefs or political views are, be tolerant. For example, when I was living in Arizona there was a bill introduced that would allow business owners to discriminate in their place of business to anyone that was part of the LGBT Community. Using social media, a vast majority of local business owners stood up and told the governor that we did not support this bill. Many businesses even started to show their solidarity by posting signs in their windows and posting Gay Pride flags on their social media walls. Tolerance to other humans can make your business relatable or boycotted. Your choice. Everyone's money is green. Next time you are faced with a controversial decision, err on the side of humanity. It's great for business and karma.

PERSEVERANCE PAYS

M ORE THAN JUST passion and talent alone perseverance pays. If you don't believe me just ask Madonna. Critics tore her apart. They said she couldn't dance, sing or act. Tell that to her 2013 banker who watched her become a billionaire. Madonna was not even considered for Evita until she wrote to the director explaining why she was the ONLY one that could play that part. She learned the score, trained her voice and mastered the tango before arriving on set. Don't let others tell you what you can do. Just do it!

CHAPTER 4

Time Management, Efficiency, Production & Organization

HAVE A TRAVEL PLAN

HAVING AN ON the road business plan will save you time, money and make you more effective. You left for a business trip with all the intentions of it being the most productive use of your time, but how many times have you left to realize that you have been gone for 5 days and accomplished only 9 hours of work in total? We have all been there. Travel is distracting. Here are a few rules that will make your travel time super productive. Forget alcohol and get good sleep. Have a plan for each day with a list of what needs to be accomplished. And if you want to read on the plane, don't pack ANY other distractions! Start each day with a to do list and end each night creating one for tomorrow.

PLANES, TRAINS & AUTOMOBILES

IF YOU ARE a Carpreneur (work from your car) or travel frequently for business - get strategic with your transport. Let's start with driving. Multi-Tasking while you are the driver is not recommended. However, this is a great opportunity to listen to ambient music, binaural beats (said to enhance creativity & intuition, and helps in stress reduction) or listen to educational audio books that you select prior. These are great things to do on your plane ride as well and can be downloaded ahead of time to avoid requiring an internet connection. If you need to travel between cities, consider taking the train or bus which is easier and provides more time to work in comfort versus a busy, loud airport or sitting in traffic. My train rides from San Diego to Los Angeles are often my most productive and creative times.

STOP PROCRASTINATING, NOW!

IF THIS IS a problem for you schedule every minute of every day. From personal tasks to professional deadlines, make sure that every commitment is accounted for in your schedule. The more of a procrastinator you are the stricter your schedule needs to be. Have it visible in printed format and digital alerts set to keep you on track. Then, commit to adhere to your own rules. An entrepreneur without self-control is fooling himself that success is on the way.

DO THE HUSTLE

B ECAUSE THEIR HUSTLE will beat your talent if your talent doesn't hustle. For example, 4 months ago my husband had no career. He had the same talent he does right now however no one knew about it but me. Instead of just practicing at home and studying at night he began peddling his Original Music Scores to any film producer that would have him. He could have waited until after graduation. Many do. But his coach taught him that hustle wins the game. Now, he is working on two full lengths films and is reaching top three in the global charts for classical music on Reverb Nation.

FILL YOUR CALENDAR

M Y BUSINESS FOR profit suffered when I stopped doing free consults. Once I had over 100 testimonials/ endorsements (2012), I felt I had proven myself and I would no longer work for free. Boy was I stupid. I asked my mentor - How do I make more money like you? He said, "Show me your calendar." My mentor showed me HIS calendar. Booked from 7am to 6pm Monday- Friday plus trade shows, events evenings and weekends. I looked at mine. Three prospects that week. He said "Gia even if you were a terrible salesperson which you are not how many sales would you close per week if you booked 20 appointments? He made his point. I started filling my calendar by offering free consults. It paid off.

WHAT BY WHEN

I T IS NEARLY impossible to achieve anything great without a plan. And a plan without a deadline is just a concept. The best way to ensure a goal is materialized is to create a list of all the tasks that need to be done for the project to be a success. Assign a WHAT (the task) by WHEN (the due date) to ensure your ultimate and timely success. Create a what by when commitment log in the notes section in the back of this book. I've left plenty of room for lots of successes!

INSIST MEETINGS BE PRODUCTIVE

P RODUCTIVE MEETINGS ALWAYS have someone leading them. Most people roll their eyes when someone suggests a "meeting." The reason for this is that most meetings are utterly useless and more of a brainstorm session than an action oriented what by when session. My tips for creating a successful meeting are the following:

1.   Have a detailed agenda.
2.   Have a leader that keeps everyone on point.
3.   Shelve great ideas unrelated to the topic at hand for a later time.
4.   Assign tasks with due dates to people in and outside of the meeting.
5.   Play musical chairs every 30 minutes. This will help the body's blood flow and keep everyone energized.

BE ON TIME

YOU SPEND A lot of time building trust and rapport with your customers. Don't erode that trust by not respecting their time. Nothing bothers me more than someone not showing up or showing up 20 or more minutes late for a meeting with no message or request for a reschedule. Just as you feel irritated with your doctor's office when you are waiting 45 minutes for a scheduled appointment, your client/colleague is irked by your lack of professionalism and respect. No one is perfect, but courtesy goes a long way.

FINISHED TRUMPS PERFECT

SPEED TO MARKET is typically more important than perfection to market. Apple is the perfect example of this. Your latest iPhone Upgrade: it's not perfect, in fact if you just wait for the second version of the model to come out, most of the glitches will be fixed. But we don't wait, we run. We do not care about perfection. We want it now. The same is true for your target client. Get your 90% project to the marketplace and they will help you figure out the 10% much more quickly than you would have on your own.

AVOID THE INTERNET RABBIT HOLE

ONE OF THE biggest productivity killers is clicking for hours on the internet getting buried in the mundane. In fact, many other people's businesses are relying on you to keep clicking on that button instead of creating valuable marketing and content that others will want to click on. Just because you are "on the computer all day" does not mean you are productive all day. Remember, news stories and videos are like potato chips, you can't eat just one.

HAVE A "TO DON'T" LIST

FROM BAD HABITS to working below your pay grade just saying no will open better opportunities to say yes to. When people hear that I have 100+ clients and members they ask HOW I can possibly manage it all and a balanced life. It is because I DON'T do: my own taxes, administrative functions, daily cash flow reports or anything that I am not fast or great at. On busy days I don't do my own cleaning or cooking. Keeping a "to - don't" list ensures that my "to do" list is filled with activities that I enjoy and am most effective completing.

MASTER YOUR TECHNOLOGY

IT CAN ENSLAVE you. Your unread mail should only serve the purpose of a to do List. If it is sitting in there, action is required. You can create folders to file and organize other emails. Determine two times per day that you will respond to emails. In those moments silence your phone. Stick to the task at hand. This method ensures productivity.

TURN OFF YOUR PHONE

SOME TASKS REQUIRE your full concentration and focus. These tasks are not suited to be done while multi-tasking. For example: writing is something that will require extra attention and a clear mind. A buzzing or vibrating phone simply serves as a distraction. Even if you don't answer it your mind is still considering what/who the call may have been about. Set aside quiet times during the day when you can drill down into the details without disturbance.

DO IT IN THE MOMENT

MAKING LISTS IS great however some things are better done in the moment. If you have 28,000 emails in your inbox how exactly do you cull out the 2 sales and 15 hot leads in a timely manner? You don't. Marketing a business that is a hot mess is a waste of time. Get organized.

WORK AHEAD

IF YOU HAVE ever done a bunch of work right before vacation you know how much you can get done! For example: if I am on a creative roll with one of my client's advertising and content is flowing I won't just do what is due for today I will continue while I am in that flow and do as much as I can until I become tired. I can get a month's worth of work done in half the time when doing it in the "zone".

STOP RELYING ON MEMORY

EVEN A PHOTOGRAPHIC memory is no match compared to your iPhone calendar complete with alerts. If you are like most small business owners and Entrepreneurs, you are checking your phone 10-14 times per hour. There is no gadget that takes more of your attention. This is a good thing. If you are religious about entering every prospect call, meeting, sales call and customer service calls the likelihood of missing something important shrinks. I only schedule appointments via text. This keeps everything on a calendar in one place, my iPhone.

CLEAN YOUR DESK

A DISORDERLY DESK CAN be the cause of a lack of focus. It is difficult to be productive amidst workspace chaos. Start or end each day by cleaning your desk completely and wiping it down. Then organize and prioritize the contents. Review your to do list for the day, and create a new one for tomorrow. A clutter free desk allows you to be more persistent and less frustrated according to a recent Harvard Business Review study.

CHAPTER 5

Research, Sales, Marketing & Measurability

KNOW YOUR MARKET

I F YOU DON'T know who your market is how will you know where to find them? For example: if your audience is under 18 and you are only focusing your marketing efforts on Facebook you are making a mistake. Facebook's demographics are 18-65 with the heaviest of the bulk between 20 and 64. Perfect if you are targeting Gen X and Baby Boomers. But if you want to catch the younger generation you'll find them on Instagram and Snapchat. Look to your sales/customers. Those are the demographics that matter.

LEARN YOUR CLIENT'S INDUSTRY

THAT MEANS RESEARCHING and staying on top of trends one of my clients is a Plastic Surgeon. He has issued me an "honorary plastic surgery" degree. His posts are filled with knowledge and expertise. He doesn't have 10 hours a week to train me. Instead every day I learn something new about plastic surgery. Something I can share with his patients and prospects. No matter what you do for your customer, make sure you go the distance in getting to know their business. I knew nothing about estate planning or business taxes until I had to educate myself properly to serve my clients.

LOOK YOUR BEST

DOING BUSINESS IS a lot like dating. You have .003 seconds to get their attention. Will your branding reel them in in that short amount of time? It should. I've seen people spend thousands of dollars on print advertising and minimal money on their branding or even worse no money on their branding and have hand-made, third grade looking artwork. When I had a story in the business journal, my website got an additional 21 hits that day. On the average my posts on social media are seen by over 1,000,000+ people per month. In short, rethink your advertising budget. And take social media as seriously as you would a billboard on the main intersection in your town.

BE YOUR PRODUCT

A SMART MAN ONCE told me "I don't watch people's lips, I watch their feet". It doesn't matter what you say if you do not walk your talk. If you are selling weight loss be fit. If you are a lung cancer surgeon, don't smoke cigarettes. It's like my grandmother used to say: "If you want a friend, be a friend". If you are a hairstylist, your hair should look impeccable daily. If you are a financial advisor, you should be financially set or well on your way. If you are not where you need to be find a mentor that has already achieved success in your industry.

STAY RELEVANT

WITH GOOGLE ALERTS you can keep your finger on the pulse of breaking news in your industry. Just because you were a certified public accountant genius in 1979 doesn't mean you are a genius today. It doesn't matter which industry you work in or what product or service you sell. Stay on top of the trends and new technologies emerging by setting up alerts and researching new advances in your area of expertise. Never rest on your laurels when it comes to knowledge in your industry or the new kids will kick you right off the block.

DON'T MISTAKE MARKETING FOR SALES

MARKETING IS GETTING eyeballs on your business. Sales is getting those eyeballs to buy from you. Without marketing and sales working together, no one knows you exist and they never hire you. When using social media marketing, your job is to get as many eyeballs of your target audience as possible, then educate them and make them an irresistible offer. Because social media is referral based marketing, trying to sell directly from this platform can isolate your customer. Instead, use social media to drive your customer to a call to action that ends with a salesperson. This brings return on your investment.

STOP SELLING

WHEN SPEAKING IN front of entrepreneurs I ask them to raise their hands if they want me to teach them how to sell on Facebook. All the hands go up. I then reveal (to shocked faces) that I won't be teaching them to sell on Facebook. When we "sell" people we get complaints and cancellations. When we "magnetize" our customers we get reviews and endorsements.

HOW TO MAGNETIZE YOUR SALES

S TEPS TO MAGNETIZE:

1. Define your target audience. Who do you help?
2. Look good, have branding that gets their attention and focuses on what THEY want not who YOU are.
3. Educate first through your posts and then give them a call to action.
4. Give them knowledge on a webinar, phone call or meeting.
5. Give them options to work with you. Those who select to work with you have been magnetized, not sold.

DON'T SELL TO JERKS

N O MATTER HOW much you need the money. If you think about the biggest jerks you have served, you can probably agree that you knew from the moment you met them that they were trouble. When someone shows you who they are, believe them.

SHOOT FOR THE STARS

EVEN IF YOU only make it to Venus you'll be a huge hit. Beware of the people in your life that tell you to be "realistic". Trust me Steve Jobs, Bill Gates and Martin Luther King Jr., all had these "realists" in their life. However, in order to reach our full potential and inspire others to do the same we must aim as high as we can in everything we do. Like the wise sage Bloody Mary in South Pacific sang "If you don't have a dream, how you going to have a dream come true?"

BE YOUR OWN CHEERLEADER

SOME PEOPLE ARE too humble to call themselves an "expert" or announce their accolades to the market or prospective clients. I say they are doing more harm than good by not vocalizing their capabilities and successes. If you were applying for a job at a Fortune 500 company, they would expect you to tell them in full detail all of your accomplishments. What you have done in the past gives them an idea of what you can bring to their company. The same is true with being a small business owner. You must market yourself (or hire someone else to) daily or hourly if you want to have consistent business. In the past, eight to ten touches were necessary to close a customer. Today, it takes somewhere between 80-120 interactions.

REGARDING SOCIAL MEDIA

UNLESS YOU ARE getting massive engagement, work on getting one post per day to go viral. No more. No less. I see business owners putting up multiple posts in one day with zero engagement on the posts. It is like running into a forest by yourself and screaming at the top of your lungs all day. This behavior is exhausting for sure and not very fruitful. Work on engaging one post per day in each platform you choose to engage in. This will yield far better results.

VET YOUR EXPERTS

THEY MAY BE living in a van, down by the river. The last thing you want to do is hire someone that has failed to monetize their primary business but now wants the opportunity to fail to monetize yours. For example, almost everyone that was doing social marketing & PR from 2009-2012 that I knew is now working a retail job. If they don't have a litany of endorsements and testimonials from other business owners how do you know they will perform for your business?

HAVE GREAT BRANDING

I T IS ONE way to fake it until you make it. Even when I lost it all in the real estate crash and had to start over with pennies to my name I had great branding. I bartered my services and expertise in exchange for the same. When it comes to social media and internet marketing you have less than 1 second to get their attention before they move onto something else. Only great branding will get you that result. If you want people to regard you as the expert, you are going to need to look like it.

WEBSITE NOT OPTIONAL

E VEN IF YOU have to build one yourself. If you can't afford it there are plenty of website companies that offer free platforms for you to build a basic website until you can afford a professional one. A few recommendations from Entrepreneur Magazine: Yola, Jimdo, Google Sites & Intuit Sites.

KEEP WEBSITE SIMPLE

L ESS IS MORE when it comes to content on your website the first goal of a website is to capture their attention and email. The second goal of the website is to drive them to a call to action. In order to be successful at these actions, our branding must act as bait at the end of a fishing line. The hook must carry the pain point of your intended audience. Example, one of mine is "Using Facebook to market your business and haven't made $1? Click here for a free webinar on how to explode your business on Facebook". Make sure the opt in is above the fold (what you can see without scrolling) for best conversion.

GAIN FOLLOWERS

Y OU NEED FOLLOWERS not just in social media, but in life. True leaders have followers. If no one is following you, you are not a leader. Social media is no different than real life. If you buy your followers, they are not real but just a physical manifestation of your ego. Followers are interested in what you have to say but more important they are interested in watching what you DO. My followers predicate my next move. For example: I put a quote on my Facebook page and it got more than 12 times the normal views. So, I put up another. Even more views. This was my market's way of telling me what they wanted more from me. In return, I delivered them what they wanted.

BROADCAST LIVE ON SOCIAL MEDIA

MY TOP 2 picks are Facebook and YouTube. It doesn't have to be perfect or professionally shot it just needs to be you. In 2016, the average person on Facebook is watching 41 minutes of video per day on-site. Why should you show video on your personal wall anyway? It's called lifestyle. If I am going to make a choice between consultant A and consultant B, I will take a trip to their Facebook wall to see whose lifestyle and personality is a better match for me.

SPEAK FOR FREE

SPEAKING FOR A FEE is like having a job. Once the job is over payment ceases to exist. Speaking for free is a great way to create passive residual income. Especially if you have a yearly membership program for attendees to join. I would rather have 20 new annual clients from a free speaking gig with the average sale being $2,000 than a flat rate of $5,000 to be a paid speaker. Change your perspective on FREE!

GET THE OPRAH EFFECT

FROM VIDEOS ON Facebook to Photos on Instagram make sure they see you everywhere they look. Hired to help a political campaign I learned something that terrified me and also helped me sharpen my marketing acumen. The candidate told me that 90% of the people vote strictly on name recognition. Which lead me to believe that as long as we got this underdog's name onto the internet and social media more than his competitors, we would win. We did. The biggest upset in AZ political history. So if you really want to destroy your competitors do it with lots of content that highlights your knowledge, expertise, name, company name and face. My mentor Ira calls it "The Oprah Effect."

NETWORK, YOUR NET WORTH DEPENDS ON IT

BUT NOT JUST in person - be exponentially more successful by networking through social media. If you have a local business that depends on local traffic I strongly suggest both an in person and technological approach to networking. Combining the two equates to a home run. If your business can serve people nationally or globally, face to face networking is very limited. Make sure you have a large online network that can help take your social messages viral daily. Cultivate online "friends" the same way you would offline friends, relationships first, business second.

BUILD RELATIONSHIP KARMA

I HAVE A FRIEND that I know is one sharp shooter. In her business she is professional, strategic and genius. Personally, she is huge hearted, kind & warm. Exactly the kind of person I want in my life forever. I knew she could use my program. I knew that it would drive more eyeballs to her business. So, I gifted her a $3,000 membership. Subsequently, a few weeks later she introduced me to a group that has decided to have me as their opening speaker on social media after interviewing me. Relationship Karma. Who have you blessed lately?

FOCUS ON THE PEOPLE WHO "GET IT"

THERE ARE THREE types of people. Those who naturally get it, those who want to get it and those whom will never get it. Sometimes our ego wants to fight harder to win over people that will "never get it". We need to become competent and trusting enough with our intuitive side to see the difference. Then, we must be courageous enough to walk away when we know the person before us will "never get it" and ultimately does not want to "get it". Do you get it?

TWO BIRDS, ONE STONE

D O YOU PROMOTE TWO businesses pages on social media? If so this is a nifty trick. When posting on one page use the "Check in" feature to "tag" your other business. This will put the post on page one into the public, while also creating a secondary link to the 2nd page. Did that sound like a IKEA instruction booklet? Check out the "What's Next" section at the back of this book.

CHAPTER 6

Money in, Money Out

EASE UP ON YOUR PRICING

SOMETIMES I HAVE to tell a client that if the only price point they have is five to ten thousand dollars, then they will be eliminating a massive amount of opportunities. Offering financing on larger amounts or offering services that are a lesser value that take up less of your time is a great way to make money and build relationships at every turn.

WORK FOR FREE

UNTIL YOU HAVE enough endorsements, testimonials and case studies to quantify your cost, work for free. From 2009-2011 I created a networking group that met regularly and taught them Facebook Marketing all for free even though I was broke. By the time I started charging in 2011, we had a line of over 60 people waiting to sign up because of the success we created with the "free" members for two years. If you do not have the gumption to work for free my guess is that your passion level is not high enough for the career, you have chosen. Because even WITH these endorsements, I still work for free when prospecting a new client, giving a workshop or a free consultation.

START A MEMBERSHIP

MEMBERSHIP IS CONSISTENT income for my business. I worked for free for two years while I built my name alongside my success stories. When I started charging it was $50 per month. From there I added VIP Private coaching & branding and raised my price to $100 per month. Having affordable options has kept me with volume business, producing well over 6 figures for over 5 years. You can do this too. Start free and gather evidence of success. As you gain more evidence of success, the worth of your product will continuously rise.

STOP SLASHING YOUR PRICES

ONCE YOU HAVE measurable proof of your success, stop bargaining. Most people don't pick the cheapest anyway, they pick the best value for the money. So give them value. Check out what your competitors are charging and what they are delivering. If you are delivering more value than your competitors, then your price can be higher. If you are delivering less value than your rivals, you have an opportunity to step your game up. Accepting a low ball offer (if your pricing is fair) tells the universe (verbally & energetically) your real bottom line. Case studies, endorsements and testimonials are a MUST in proving value.

COUNT COSTS BEFORE COMMITTING

SURE IT'S A great idea but you need to figure out if you can afford it before you commit to it. I'm not just speaking of the financial costs. You also need to decide if you have the time, energy and passion required for the task at hand. How many times have you committed to something today that you wish you could get out of tomorrow? Commitment is huge and it should be. It is your word, your bond, your promise to deliver on something. Want your clients to be loyal to you? Earn their loyalty over time by keeping your commitments.

PAY BY THE JOB, NOT BY THE HOUR

PAYING HOURLY EMPLOYEES can break the bank pretty quickly. I have saved thousands of dollars paying people by the project instead of by the hour. I learned this in the construction industry in Mexico. In the morning the contractor would measure where the job was. At quitting time, they would measure the progress and pay accordingly. You can't imagine how productive people become when motivated financially to be so.

HIRE AN ACCOUNTANT

BEFORE YOU ARE making "real money". Setting up a system for account billable and receivables is crucial early on. It will avoid having to pay costly fees later on when they have to try to make sense of what you have done. Hiring a brilliant tax accountant has saved me tens of thousands of dollars annually.

CHAPTER 7

Stay Relevant, Practice Leadership & Gratitude

STUDY & SPREAD LEADERSHIP

IF YOU REALLY want to grow your company, you will also have to grow yourself alongside it. There is no shortcut to success without leadership. First of all, your entire corporate culture will be a reflection of the leadership within. Second, if you want your company to be respected YOU will have to be respected first. Leadership maximizes productivity and promotes harmony in any corporation. Subsequently monies invested into leadership training and books will without a doubt bring in a return on investment as a side benefit to the other gains.

BE A SOCIALPRENEUR

CREATE A BUSINESS that will remedy a societal problem while still turning a profit. For every $10,000 my company earns in helping business owners realize their marketing dreams we donate $2,000 in services to a deserving and needy struggling entrepreneur or business owner. Giving away 20% helps my company as much as it helps my heart. How can you become a socialpreneur today?

BE THE CHANGE

ONLY THEN CAN you SPREAD the change. For example: I have experienced many companies advertising that they sell "social media marketing". Upon further review of their social sites they have failed to do a good job creating their own buzz. If they cannot prove success marketing their own business how will they succeed with yours? Don't buy from anyone that has failed to prove success for themselves.

KNOW WHAT TRUST IS

TRUST IS ACCOUNTABILITY over time. When people ask you to "Trust" them, remind them of this formula. You may have faith but trust needs to be earned. What is the best way to have faith in a stranger you are considering doing business with? Check out their endorsements, referrals & testimonials. Never trust someone you don't have time with. Let them prove why you should have faith based on the trust of others they have worked with.

ADMIT FLAWS AND MISTAKES

WHEN YOU DO, you gain trust, credibility and even help from those around you. Everyone knows that no one is perfect. As long as you take responsibility for your mistakes and make amends where needed mistakes are OK. In fact, they are inevitable. Leaders are not paralyzed by mistakes because they know that every mistake breeds an opportunity for learning. In fact, sometimes a mistake can lead to a huge discovery that you would not have found otherwise. So embrace the mistakes because they are a part of success.

BUILD THEIR TRUST

EVERYTHING YOU DO with a client is either building or breaking trust. From a phone call to a meeting. Take that seriously. Gaining their business does not necessarily mean you have earned their trust. And even if they trust you initially they could lose this trust later on. Build their trust by keeping impeccable records of what you promised them (with a due date) and then deliver them on time. If you are going to be two minutes late or more for a scheduled meeting, text or call ahead out of courtesy. An apology is appreciated, but correcting the issue onward is atonement.

BE THE SAME WITH EVERYONE

IF YOU HAVE a weekend personality, a work personality and a church personality, you might be schizophrenic. You're not actually fooling anyone. In fact, they are probably talking about your inconsistencies behind your back. Embrace your true self without any apology. Sure, some people may not like you but at least you know the ones that stick around really do. If you find parts of your life too tawdry for public consumption, you may need to question why you are doing it. If you can't have it posted on the front of the NY Times, you probably shouldn't be doing it.

CAREFUL WHOM YOU HIRE

P ROCEED WITH CAUTION when hiring associates & employees - your success depends on them. When I was in my 20s, I was interviewed over 4 times by the same company for the same position. First there were 10 of us being interviewed in this fashion. Then 7. Then 4. Then 2. I thought this was insane. Now, I understand this is how top level organizations function. They test your patience to see how you work under pressure over time. Couple this with a trial period and you can avoid a money pit of negative experiences.

ENGAGE IN GRATITUDE

S HOW APPRECIATION FOR the things you have instead of griping about the things you don't have. Being sad and obsessing on what you do not have is almost like praying for it to continue. Expressing gratitude for what you do have immediately counteracts the negative thoughts. Try to start or end your day with what you are grateful for. This practice has a knack for bringing more things to be grateful for. Starting a gratitude journal would be a great way to incorporate this aspect in your life.

SEND HANDWRITTEN NOTES

WHEN WE RECEIVE a handwritten note it triggers a physiological response that creates happiness. While a complete digital environment in this day and age is best for your business I make the exception for thank you notes. A thank you email just doesn't quite hit the mark. Whether I am prospecting or offering thanks to a current friend, colleague or client, I use stationery, a pen and heartfelt words. Everyone loves them. Consider a custom stamp with your company logo.

ASK FOR REFERRALS & TESTIMONIALS

YOUR HAPPY AND satisfied customers stories are better than any bragging you can say about yourself. Also, don't be shy to ask for their referrals. Chances are their friends and family are also your target client. You can ask for these referrals in person, by email, snail mail or through your social media postings. Make sure that you have some kind of bonus or gift of gratitude for these referrals even if it is just a handwritten note. You want to thank them for their support of your small business.

CHAPTER 8

Mentors, Strategic Alliances & Contractors Oh Me!

STOP BEING A LONEPRENEUR

JUST AS IT takes a village to raise a child, it takes a team to create a successful company. That doesn't mean you need a ton (or even any) employees. But collaborators, contractors and colleagues can fill in the gaps in your business. Keeping others in your circle for brainstorming, planning, sharing of costs and experiences can nurture your business. Make sure your online network is as powerful as our Face to Face network for maximum results.

CREATE STRATEGIC ALLIANCES

THEY CAN BE short term or last for years. Many entrepreneurs and small business owners do not want a partner in their business. I get that I really do. However, I would be nowhere today if it were not for my strategic alliances. From graphics firms to mentors to business coaches and more my strategic alliances make me look good and help bring in and maintain business. And in turn I keep them flush with business as well.

JOIN YOUR LOCAL CHAMBER

NETWORKING IS GREAT for building local business relationships. Local chambers are great for connecting with other small business owners. When interacting, first ask them about **their business.** If you are looking to meet bigger executives from larger corporations try to join service or philanthropic oriented clubs like the Lions Club International. The more successful tend to avoid networking in lieu of doing good deeds. Learn from them.

HAVE A MENTOR

I BANGED MY HEAD against the wall for months with a work issue. I sat down for 30 seconds with my mentor Bill Walsh and he was solving my problem before I was done speaking it. My mentor is a multi-million-dollar deal maker. I offered to be a part of his team & help spread the good word about his organization. This gave me the opportunity to spend more time with him. Every time I was near him a new pearl of wisdom would be discovered. Find someone in your field that has 10Xs more success than you do and work with and/or for them. Visit www. success2020.com now and hear Bill live in your city.

EVEN TIGER WOODS HAS A COACH

NO MATTER HOW good you are, there is someone that can help you get to great. Sure you could do it all yourself. But, think about it this way, after New Year's many sign up for the gym to help achieve their New Year's Resolutions only to never show up again. In fact, the gyms count on it. It is how they sell 40,000 memberships to a facility that can only house up to 400 people at a time. However, those that sign up with a personal trainer have a far greater chance of showing up for their scheduled appointments. Who is coaching you?

LISTEN TO YOUR PAID EXPERTS

INSANITY IS PAYING experts and then ignoring their advice. I watched my mentor tell his $100,000 student what to do when she took that stage. I watched her take the stage and do the exact opposite of what he said. I had to pull him out of the room to ask him if she was INSANE. He said everyone pays him the $100,000 for that level of coaching and only 10% actually follow his advice. Be smart. Listen to your experts.

ADD THE OPPOSITE SEX

INTO YOUR BUSINESS and inject it with new life. When I first started creating and hosting networking events I started with 100% women. The reason for this was simple: women network and build relationships better than most men. In fact, many published reports show that the largest marketplace in the world, Facebook, is dominated by women. Conversely, adding men and more masculine energy into my networking groups created a more dynamic environment. Yin and yang, male and female energies when combined correctly can serve more than when apart.

DON'T BE A DINOSAUR, MENTOR A MILLENNIAL

INFUSE YOUR BUSINESS with an all new energy, while helping mold the future generation. The future is now. This year Millennials officially outnumber Baby Boomers as the largest living generation. Those born during this period were born with the internet in their pockets. They do not remember a life without social media. Like Princess Leia to Obie-Wan Kenobi, the Millennials are your only hope. They are our future leaders and future business owners. Don't let them crush your business with their internet savvy & social prowess. Adopt one and make him or her your own. Evolve or die.

YOU CANNOT DO it alone. This is one thing I will guarantee you. From the women that raised me, to the mentors that taught me and clients that praise me, these bonus tips and tactics are from people I admire for various reasons. I hope they inspire and motivate you as well. Their contact information has been provided because they are committed to helping other entrepreneurs reach their dreams.

MERIA HELLER – MERIA.net
(Mother, CEO, News Personality, Podcaster)

How to Be a Spectacular Podcaster

"I'm interesting because I'm interested"

I'VE BEEN A successful podcaster since I began my show in 2000 with an audience of 15!

Remember in 2000 most computers didn't have speakers and very few were aware of what was then called "webcasts".

Today my show is international with thousands upon thousands of listeners and listener supported. I produce and host the longest running podcast on the net.

I've always been interested in learning and knowing everything about everything. I was taught great study habits by my father and I thank him every day for that. I estimate I've done about 5,000 shows and yet I manage to keep them interesting and the audience coming back. I learned things about subjects I never wanted to know about. I tailored my shows towards what I intuitively felt my audience would find interesting. It was what I was interested in!

A big mistake by many newbies in podcasting is they are a "one trick pony". Let's face it how many shows can you do on roses and keep your audience coming back? If you aren't a good speaker, you can consider vocal training. Nothing turns off an audience more than an annoying voice or inflection.

Have a sense of humor. Many an ugly truth can be delivered with humor. The old adage "a teaspoon of sugar helps the medicine go down" is true.

Figure out who your audience is. Then use social media to round them up. If you're not using social media, don't even bother with a podcast. No one will know it exists.

Be available to the newbies in the form of interviews or guidance. I have openly shared how I do my podcast, the equipment and costs concerned and even my guests! That's how the buzz starts traveling about you! Sharing and caring. I have a successful subscription service to my show. I also promote them with snippets on YouTube, Facebook, etc.

After 17 years on the net I am introduced as "The Godmother of the Internet" or "The Internet Legend". It could happen to you too!

www.Meria.net
The Meria Heller Show
17 Years on the net, for good reason!

ROSE RUBINO – SHOWCASES
(Aunt, CEO, Packaging & Distribution company)

Pay attention to their successes but pay more to their failures

I WORKED FOR OTHER people for many years. My bosses considered me their greatest asset. I am and was dependable, systematic and could find a solution to any problem. Delegating and managing others was my specialty and because of those skills I was able to grow exponentially as I created an assembly line system of success in each industry I touched.

I have always been financially successful and well invested but by 1990 I had enough of going back and forth between being a worker and being an entrepreneur. Since then, I have created a mega successful business that specializes in one target audience. Librarians.

My advice is to find something that is needed in the marketplace and create a solution for it. (A solution that exceeds all of the solutions that have come before it.) My next piece of advice is to get rid of all the naysayers in your world. Listen only to those that are more successful than you are.

My last piece of advice is to watch everyone around you closely. Don't just study their successes though. The real education is in their failures. I have learned more cumulatively from the failures of others than I have from their successes. In addition, failure builds experience and character. It encourages the strong and discourages the weak.

LINDA D'AURIA – WINTER PARK DINER
(CEO, Restauranteur)

Start from the bottom up - it's the best way to learn

ALL MY LIFE for as long as I can remember I have been in the service industry. As a little girl I remember volunteering at community events with my father and going behind the scenes to help serve food. Then as a teenager I was the candy girl at the local movie theatre. Whether it was for free or profit I loved the smiles and gratitude that came along with serving up delicious foods. I guess I have always been a foodie.

My passion and work ethic gave rise to management offers at every establishment I have ever worked at: from movie theatres to family owned/run restaurants and local community delis. I have always loved being "Linda" behind the counter, the person that knew everyone's name and favorite dishes.

The Winter Park Diner has been a staple in the greater Orlando area since 1956 and in 1988 with the help of my real estate profits and sister/investor, I became the proud new owner. As sexy as it sounds it has been without a doubt the most difficult profession I probably could have chosen but one of the most rewarding. I am now a pillar in the community, a commercial real estate property owner and in a very good position for my one-day retirement.

However, life wasn't like that right away. I have paid my dues and then some. Anyone starting a business that is doing it for more vacations needs to think again. It was 2 years with no salaries and back breaking work that paved the road for future success. We have been through several recessions, but thanks to our loyal followers and affordable pricing, we are always the last to feel it. You better be tough. At one point I was a single mother working the hot kitchen all day, taking care of my mother plagued with cancer, raising my nephew and supporting all of us on $150 a week. When you own a business and people are relying on you for their life, no matter what is going on, you have to do what is right for your business. It takes a big set to be an entrepreneur.

IRA ROSEN – MOJO MARKETING GLOBAL
(Founder of over 300+ medical weight loss centers
& CEO of a Global Marketing Organization)

Selling anything is a numbers game

FIFTY YEARS AGO selling was a numbers game and fifty years from now it will still be a numbers game. Gia mentions it in previous pages. Show me your calendar and I show you how successful you are at acquiring new customers. I am not saying it is easy to do this on a daily basis. You are going to need to be disciplined and relentless in your daily pursuit of interested prospects and limit all other distractions. Without prospecting and closing sales you will not last. Also our consultations are free and we are still a multi-million dollar producing business.

Need help keeping your funnel full? Visit www.MojoGlobal.com today.

BILL WALSH – POWERTEAM USA
(Mentor, Speaker, CEO & America's Best Salesman)

STOP WAITING TO start. When I Met Gia over 5 years ago, I had already heard that she was the best at Facebook so I hired her. Fortunately for me and unfortunately for her she was way underpriced. So I asked her to come speak at one of my events. I told her "you're not selling any of that $50 a month stuff at my event though. I need you to sell a 12-week training course on how business owners can use Facebook to benefit their business. Before I was finished asking, Gia was quick with her response that she did not have a 12-week training course. How could she sell something that didn't exist? So I asked her if she could show up next Wednesday on a webinar and teach the first thing they should know about Facebook. Her reply was "of course." I then asked her if she could do that the following week. "Easy" she replied. That weekend Gia sold five $3000 packages. Instead of five $50 packages. So the moral of the story is, start faster and never undervalue your services.

Visit www.Rainmakersystem.net/startnow if you want to learn how to increase your income.

JEFFREY MEYERSON - THE MEYERSON FIRM
(CEO, Estate Planning & Business Law Attorney)

The Magical Formula for Success After Law School!

SORRY TO BE the one to tell you, there is no magic or secret in starting your own law firm out of law school or after a few years at another firm. The main key to success is being good at what you do. Unless you are in an area of law that relies heavily on TV and print advertising, the quality of your work and perception of the value you offer will determine whether people refer work to you and whether clients will stay with you.

It took me 7 years of working in large law firms to feel comfortable working on projects without partner supervision. I recognized early in my career that I didn't know nearly as much as I needed to, so I stayed in the big firm environment until I did.

That doesn't mean that you can't start your own firm straight out of law school. It means that you will need to spend a lot of time researching issues and learning the nuances of your chosen area of law.

Establishing a network of quality attorneys that are willing to help can shorten the learning curve. Recognizing your limitations and asking for help is a great way to learn. There are a lot of small firm attorneys that are willing to co-counsel on matters that are beyond your experience.

Understanding your market and where your clients come from is another key.

You have to be willing to develop and implement a strategic plan. I spent a lot of time trying to find professionals roughly my same age that were respected in their industries and that I could grow with professionally over time.

The process is frustrating and the peaks and valleys early on can be frightening especially if you have a family. If you can push through that stage and continue establishing your networks, things begin to even out.

Also, it helps if people like you. People do business with people they like and trust. So above all else, don't ever be a jerk. Learn all you ever wanted to know about wills and trusts here and keep up with the latest news and updates in estate planning;
www.Facebook.com/PhoenixWillsAndTrusts

MICHAEL HOWARD – ORIGINAL MUSIC SCORES
(Composer, Film Scorer)

Stay single for success OR pick the right partner

YOU HEAR A lot of people say that it is better to stay single while you are building your career. This way the focus is on your work. I guess that makes sense for people that are not picking the right kind of partners.

Whether the relationship with your partner is for business, friendship, or love, it needs to be a constructive one. The relationship I have with my wife works because we share similar views on the world, who we want to show up in life as and our strengths complement one another perfectly.

When I met my wife I had failed out of college several times. I was working a fast-food job and had no real desire to do anything else. I thought about going to school for music but ultimately decided hanging around and doing nothing was easier. I was acting like an entitled Millennial. Something my wife absolutely hates. I had no drive and I felt that I had a lack of control over my own destiny and future.

When my wife was my girlfriend she made an ultimatum. I could go to the Landmark Education Forum or I could lose her number forever. I chose Landmark. And what I didn't know was that meant I was going to be choosing me. My desires. My dreams. This is my blank canvas and I can paint anything I want on it. I always had talent but I never had the confidence to believe I could write music for a living successfully.

Now, I am a straight A student at Full Sail University working on my Bachelors of Music Production. And, at the advice of my wife I am scoring a documentary pro-bono to build my resume and have started producing my own classical music which has reached #1 on the local charts and #3 in the world. So don't believe the hype on staying single to be successful. Just make sure you pick the right partner. I sure did.

JEREMY JONES - THE BOOK DISTRICT
(3 Times Best Selling Author on Amazon, Publisher)

The 20% Shift That Could Bring You 80% More Revenue

YOU'VE PROBABLY HEARD of the 80/20 rule. Marketing experts like Perry Marshall have made it popular by explaining the 80/20 rule and how it applies to sales and marketing. The rule says that 20 percent of what you do will account for 80 percent of your results. 20 percent of your time during the day will produce 80 percent of the results, and so on and so one.

There are 3 reasons why people do business with you. They know you, they like you, and they trust you...if you have been an entrepreneur for 30 seconds, and read any books related to sales and marketing chances are you've heard this before.

Here's why you need to publish a book for your startup business. Simply because it's a way to leverage your time and get more people to know you, like you and trust you while you are doing other things. If you are like me, and most people are, when you read a book you feel more connected and like the author more after reading a book (if it's good content of course). You feel like you know them, like them, and trust them (because they are an expert on the topic) much more after reading their book.

As you are reading this, it logically makes sense and I'm sure you can agree. If this idea makes sense, you'll probably want to look into other books I have, with other great simple ideas that work. If you like my ideas, you'll want to look up my blog and get more engaged with me. After you look at my blog www.AskJeremyJones.com, you'll see there that I post more free content there too. It's obvious to people, that I'm a guy that gives a ton of value first. And most people say they want to do business with me because if I give away this much great value, image how great it will be when you do business with me.

The book starts the conversation. By having a book published, not about you necessarily, but a book that solves a problem or challenge for your clients directly. A marketing book that teaches you how to generate your first 10 leads. A productivity book that teaches you how to get more done and free up an hour in your day. These non-fiction book examples are a one topic book that could lead directly into your business and what you do.

Book sales are great, they are profitable, however it's the 20% advantage you'll get by using a book with your startup. By putting a focus on a high value book for your clients, they will know you, like you, and trust you much faster.

Remember the rule that says you have to make 7 contacts with a client before they do business with you? Here are 7 contacts. See a promotion, one, visit the landing page, two, order your book, three, receive the book, four, start reading the book on day one, five, finish reading the book on day two, six, then at the end of the book give a consultation, and they reach out to you, step 7 in the contacts. By the time they reach you, they already know you, like you, and trust you.

Consider writing a book, even if you don't know where to start, we can help you come up with a great idea. 82% of people say they would like to publish a book at some point in their life. The problem is, most people don't take the first step.

By promoting your business with a book that adds value first, it can be the 20% of actions you take, that start to produce 80% of your revenue... because people know you, like you and trust you and ultimately want to do business with you because you helped make their life a little better.

Learn how to build your online credibility and authority from scratch, and get a FREE copy of my #1 Best Selling Book on Amazon here: www. TheBookDistrict.com/power-authority

Jeremy C. Jones

Three-time, #1 Best Selling Author on Amazon, Military Veteran, and most importantly, Family Man. Jeremy is the founder of Jones Media Publishing, an innovative publishing company that truly is an advocate for self-published authors. His company provides coaching and support from Idea to Published. In 2015 he founded TheBookDistrict.com, a rapidly growing community for aspiring authors and published experts. Through his popular podcast and online communities, he has helped more than 7 clients reach #1 Best Seller on Amazon.

KRISTINE VOWLES – THE LUXURY LOOK
(CEO, President of the Home Staging Association)

Turn your 7 degrees of separation down a few degrees

EVERYONE IS AT least 7 degrees of separation from a major influencer in the world. I have been so successful building my links throughout the years that my connections are down to 1 – 2 degrees away from major influencers like Oprah Winfrey or Richard Branson.

Every person you meet is an opportunity. That's why I've trained my mind to work differently than most others when meeting people. Over the years I've learned to incorporate conversation in to my mind like a chain. Each chain become a link that continues to get stronger with each new conversation I have or connect to a past conversation I've stored in my memory. Because you never know who you might need to connect that person too. I have a gift of connecting, I see the value in people and my mind thinks of opportunities to connect.

For example, once I met with a Facebook friend who was excited to tell me about their new product - and was able to connect that person with three new opportunities. By linking that chain together, the income and possibilities are endless for each and every one of them. A 20-minute conversation that changed the lives of many.

It just starts with the first conversation. Who are you going to say hi to next and what will you remember about them? Connect with me at www. Facebook.com/TheLuxuryLook

Brayand Ponciano – Investor
(CEO, Real Estate Investor & House Flipper)

Believing in Yourself, even when no one else does!

WHEN I MET Gia Over 6 years ago, many people made fun of Gia because "Social Media was not serious enough to be professional" and most wrote her off as nothing more than just a fad. I was in a similar position, because I had street cred and dropped F bombs, I was dismissed by most of the business community as a flash in the pan with no real substance.

Just like I saw something special in her from day one, she immediately saw something special in me the first night we met. And because of that, she invested her heart and time into me over the years through friendship and mentorship and introductions to people like Jeff Fagin, whom has literally changed my life. Gia had already been working it for 2 years when we met, so both her online and business community reputation grew quickly; mine took a few years. Regardless, neither one of us ever stopped believing in ourselves. People talked about our unconventional asses regularly, but at the end of the day they could not deny the results that we both were producing.

As a Successful Real Estate Investor and House Flipper, I now appreciate having an example like Gia who I could look up to for inspiration on being myself regardless of what people said. Now as a successful Businessman, being myself in all my fouled mouth glory, is one of the things my Investors like most about doing business with me.

Never forget that what others think of you is unimportant. What you think of you is crucial for success, so feed your mind and your soul and evolve. Then, when you do make it, make sure to always believe in others and inspire them to Greatness as Gia did for me!

DR. ROBERT BONILLAS – SCOTTSDALE PLASTICS

(Medical Director/Founder of Scottsdale Plastics)

Starting a Medical Practice (Just a Few Tips to Get You Going)

MEDICAL SCHOOL PREPARES you to be a physician, it doesn't prepare you to start a business, yet alone, manage your medical practice. This is where helpful tips from those who have been there and done that become very helpful. Here it goes....

First and foremost, if you can't decide where you want to practice, choose a location where you want to live, and the rest will flourish. This is probably the single most important decision in your career, since most of those who do well also love where they live.

Secondly, "Go Big or Go Home" is not a slogan you should follow... initially. "Less is More" is appropriate. I have seen many practices fail within their first few years due to the amount of debt and overhead accumulated in establishing a grand practice. Office sharing is one example of how to cut down on overhead by sharing rent and office expenses. However, keep your practices separate so when you have become established, you can easily move on without major separation catastrophes.

Thirdly, be seen and be heard. Just because you open your office, have some ads and a website doesn't mean patients will find you. Attend various events in your area and don't stop. The more people see you and associate you with your specialty, the more likely they will think of you when they or a friend and/or family member needs your services. In other words, never stop networking!

Fourthly, social media and online presence has become a game changer in business recognition, and will only become more important as time goes on. However, without the expert help of a social media guru such as Gia Heller from the Social Media Masters, establishing a social media presence would be mediocre at best.

And last, but not least, work on your bedside manner. One of my strengths that I feel has solidified most of my patient relationships, and kept them from going elsewhere, is my genuine demeanor and caring bedside manner. Patients like to know that you care and you will be around when they need you. Good luck!

Robert G. Bonillas, M.D.
Aesthetic & Reconstructive Plastic Surgery
Medical Director/Founder, Scottsdale Plastics
Diplomate, The American Board of Plastic Surgery
(480) 245-6380 www.ScottsdalePlastics.com
Visit us on Facebook! www.Facebook.com/ScottsdalePlastics

ABOUT THE AUTHOR

"I've been using social media to get what I want
since 1995 and you can too!"

GIA HELLER BEGAN using social media in 1995 to jump-start her social life. Ten years later, she had expanded her network to her real estate business. Using only social media, she was able to turn the trust and credibility she earned with her clients into millions of dollars' worth of property sales. As former Marketing & Research Director at CB Richard Ellis' Retail Corporate Services, her marketing background is long proven and award winning.

When Gia first recognized that Facebook could be used to promote business and establish brand loyalty with customers, people ridiculed her. Today Gia has the last laugh: Fortune 500 companies and small businesses alike have come to use Facebook for branding and advertising.

Gia has taught thousands of entrepreneurs how to maximize their Facebook marketing and has collected over 3,000 testimonials & endorsements. She has created a collaborative community of like-minded entrepreneurs who are committed to promoting within the network. Her mission is to empower over one million entrepreneurs with the skills they need to succeed!

Next Steps

START BUILDING BUZZ around your business today! Email Gia@TheSocialMediaMasters.com for a training video and learn how to become the credible celebrity in your industry. Become a member of our online group of entrepreneurs and small business owners committed to helping market each other's businesses.

After you review the webinar, you may text
HELP A STARTUP
to **480-258-1392** to set an appointment with
www.TheSocialMediaMasters.com

Show your receipt of purchase for
The Startup Entrepreneur
And receive a *scholarship towards
services or training valued at $250.00
*May not be combined with any other offers

Connect with Gia on the following social platforms
www.Facebook.com/GiaHeller
www.Facebook.com/TheSocialMediaMasters
www.Facebook.com/TheStartupEntrepreneur
www.Instagram.com/GiaHeller
www.Linkedin.com/in/giaheller

Want to connect with other Entrepreneurs &
Business Owners in my Facebook Group?

JOIN:
www.Facebook.com/Groups/TheStartupEntrepreneur/
www.Facebook.com/Groups/FriendsOfGiaHeller

The Startup Entrepreneur

_____

_____

_____

_____

_____

_____

_____

_____

_____

_____

_____

_____

_____

_____

_____

_____

_____

_____

_____

_____

Gia Heller

Gia Heller

Gia Heller

_____

_____

_____

_____

_____

_____

_____

_____

_____

_____

_____

_____

_____

_____

_____

_____

www.ingramcontent.com/pod-product-compliance
Lightning Source LLC
Chambersburg PA
CBHW062010200326
41519CB00017B/4749